The Intensive Retreat for Couples

The Intensive Retreat for Couples

Her Workbook

The Intensive Retreat for Couples

The Intensive Retreat for Couples

Her Workbook

By

Onedia N. Gage, Ph. D.

The Intensive Retreat for Couples

Other Books by Minister Onedia N. Gage

Are You Ready for 9th Grade . . . Again? A Family's Guide to Success
As We Grow Together Daily Devotional for Expectant Couples
As We Grow Together Prayer Journal for Expectant Couples
The Best 40 Days of Your Life: A Journey of Spiritual Renewal
The Blue Print: Poetry for the Soul
From Two to One: The Notebook for the Christian Couple
Her Story: Bible Study
Her Story: Daily Devotional
Her Story: The Legacy of Her Fight
Her Story: The Legacy Journal
Her Story: Prayers and Journal
ILY! A Mother Daughter Success Kit
In Her Own Words: Notebook for the Christian Woman
In Purple Ink: Poetry for the Spirit
The Intensive Retreat for Couples: His Workbook
Love Letters to God from a Teenage Girl
The Measure of a Woman: The Details of Her Soul
The Notebook: For Me, About Me, By Me
The Notebook for the Christian Teen
On This Journey Daily Devotional for Young People
On This Journey Prayer Journal for Young People
One Day More Than We Deserve Daily Devotional for the Growing Christian
One Day More Than We Deserve Prayer Journal for the Growing Christian
Promises, Promises: A Christian Novel
Tools for These Times: Timely Sermons for Uncertain Times
With An Anointed Voice: The Power of Prayer
Yielded and Submitted: A Woman's Journey for a Life Dedicated to God
Yielded and Submitted: A Woman's Journey for a Life Dedicated to God Intimate Study
Yielded and Submitted: A Woman's Journey for a Life Dedicated to God Prayers and Journal

Library of Congress

The Intensive Retreat for Couples

Her Workbook

All Rights Reserved © 2015

Onedia N. Gage

No part of this of book may be reproduced or transmitted in
Any form or by any means, graphic, electronic, or mechanical,
Including photocopying, recording, taping, or by any
Information storage or retrieval system, without the
Permission in writing from the publisher.

Purple Ink, Inc. Press

For Information address:
Purple Ink, Inc
P O Box 41232
Houston, TX 77241
www.purpleink.net
www.onediagage.com

ISBN:
978-1-939119-50-6

Printed in the United States

Her Workbook

Dedication

for

Couples

Who need direction

Who need prayer

Who need support

Who need hope

I hope to remove divorce as an option.

I pray to inspire the desire to move toward a great solution:

A Better Marriage!

The Intensive Retreat for Couples

Her Workbook

God's Word

²⁴ Therefore shall a man leave his father and his mother, and shall cleave unto his wife: and they shall be one flesh.

Genesis 2:24 (ASV)

⁶ So that they are no more two, but one flesh. What therefore God hath joined together, let not man put asunder.

Matthew 19:6 (ASV)

³² and be ye kind one to another, tenderhearted, forgiving each other, even as God also in Christ forgave you.

Ephesians 4:32 (ASV)

The Intensive Retreat for Couples

12 | Minister Gage

Dear Lord:

I thank You for this opportunity to write this project. I pray that I have pleased You in this work.

I pray that this reaches hundreds of thousands of married couples and that those couples who are not married become closer to You and even marry. I pray that the couples are able to seek You for direction and hear you clearly about the direction You want them to take in their marriage.

Dear Father, thank You for loving us. Thank You for reminding us of Your love and what to do to love others. So often the issues we have stem from not knowing that we are loved.

Lord, remind us why You led us to one another. Our paths only crossed because of Your plans. Help us to see in each other what You see in us. Help us to forgive so that the other person can feel it and know it and embrace it. Lord, remind us that You are the supplier of our love and You equip us to love others.

Dear Lord, help us to have an abundance of grace toward others, especially my husband!

Lord, I am not always right so please forgive me and my foolishness.

As women, God we need Your guidance and leadership and we need to be reminded to submit.

Lord, I praise You and worship You for the gifts and the service for which You equipped us.

Lord, I thank You for relationships, and the ability to work at them to make them relationships which pleases You. In Jesus' name, I pray!

Because You call me daughter,

Amen.

The Intensive Retreat for Couples

Dear Woman:

Marriage is hard! I understand that sentiment, however, it is possible to have a lasting marriage. Keep in mind that the divorce rate is 53%, so that means that 47% made it. How did they do it? I know that very question is one we all have asked.

Woman, do you want your marriage? Do you want your relationship? I have been there. I have decided to divorce. Does that make it a great decision? No, not necessarily. What we do know is that we are responsible for what God says for us to do.

You dreamed of marriage since your first fairytale but that fairytale does not teach us that we will work for that fairytale. What do you challenge yourself on in your marriage? In this marriage, you will have to work and work hard, especially when you do not feel like it.

You do the work because you love your husband but you are committed to and in a covenant with God. When you do not give your best to your marriage, you robbed God, rather than your husband.

I pray for your relationships. I pray for your wholeness and a healthy spirit as you work through your relationship and discover yourself within the confines of this marriage.

Woman, you are powerful, and profoundly so. Your power should be used to revive, reconcile and refresh your marriage. You may be wondering how to do that.

You do that through prayer, behavior, and attitude. You are the total package. You can win your husband over because of who you are. You could push him away because the person you are and who you are not.

You are incredible! You are awesome! You are talented! You are profound! You are a woman—the one God called for you to be the wife for your husband. You are equipped where you are called. You are prepared to have a great marriage.

You may be concerned and consumed but I want you to focus on the following:

1. Pray
2. Repent

The Intensive Retreat for Couples

3. Confess your feelings
4. Remember why you loved him in the first place
5. Commit to your marriage
6. Recommit to God for your marriage
7. Decide that you are going to be your best self in your marriage
8. Decide that your outcome is going to be pleasing to God!

I am looking forward to great outcomes for your marriage. Share your testimony with me. I can be reached at onediagage@onediagage.com, @onediangage, and on facebook. I want to know the progress you are making.

In God's Service,

Onedia N Gage

Onedia N. Gage

Table of Contents

All About Me Quiz	21
Where are We? Why are We Here?	27
The Ideal Marriage	37
Communication	45
Can You Hear Me?: Active Listening	53
Trust	63
Love	85
Respect	111
Divorce Explored	127
Fighting Fair	137
Intimacy	153
A Better Marriage	169
Tit for Tat: The Final Charge	183
Appendix:	185
Calendar for date nights and special occasions	186
Marriage Vows	188

Marriage Goals	189
Mission, Vision, and Value Statements for your marriage, family and self	190
Expectations and Heart Rules	192
Resources	194
Acknowledgements	195
About the Author	197

The Covenant

I vow to

- Listen with my heart to my husband, expecting only the best from him without the judgement of the past.
- Forgive him of all the past hurts and the pains which has inhibited our marriage.
- Love extravagantly, with all of my heart and my mind and my soul.
- Pursue him and my marriage outlandishly and outrageously.
- Nurture the health of my relationship through positive talk and thoughts.
- Consider the feelings of my husband.
- Be honest and totally transparent with my husband.
- Be honest and totally transparent with myself.
- Look forward with anticipation the best outcome for my marriage.
- Forgive yourself of all the past hurts and the pains which has inhibited our marriage.
- Remember the great times that we have had and will pursue these times again.
- Believe in my marriage and its strength.
- Believe that my marriage can survive and will be successful.
- Share my victorious testimony about the revival of my marriage.
- Avoid the negative talk about my husband and my marriage.
- Listen to my heart about my needs and desires for myself, my husband, and my marriage.

I enter this covenant with love, truth, and faith.

_____   _____
The Wife   Date

The Intensive Retreat for Couples

Instructions for Use

This journal is designed to accompany the in person retreat which I host several times each year. Whether you are in class with me or doing it alone, the results should be an improved relationship based on following the directions.

1. Read each statement and question carefully. A correct and complete understanding will lead to a better comprehension while answering and addressing those areas authentically.
2. Answer with the depths of your soul. DO NOT answer to please someone else or what you believe is more correct than what you truly feel.
3. Stay focused on the immediate topic. Use the note section for tangents.
4. Remember this is not graded, yet a living and breathing document which is simply your heart on paper.
5. DO NOT anticipate what your husband will answer, think or feel. Answer based on what you truly feel. This is an opportunity to express how you feel without the influence of your husband.
6. Be willing to see your marriage from a different, fresh, possibly different perspective.
7. Be HONEST! It is time to be honest with everyone. Your marriage depends on it.
8. Hear your husband with an open heart, prepared to forgive and renew yourself and your husband for ALL that has happened in your relationship.
9. Be prayerful. God has the first and last decision in your relationship.
10. Expect the BEST. Remain positive. Remind yourself about the positive aspects of your relationship and husband.
11. Share the positive outcomes to encourage others.

Her Workbook

Introductions

Who you are impacts your relationship. Your moods, your attitudes, your emotions, your happiness, your anger, and all attributes affect your marriage.

Your details matter! Those details drive choices your husband makes—some consciously and some unconsciously.

Below is the "All About Me" Quiz. Please complete it twice—once about him; the other is the answer key for him. Please use the last five spaces to create questions of your own.

Just a note: please share with him when the answers to the items on the quiz change.

All About Me

1. What are five of my favorite movies?
2. What is my ideal meal?
3. Where is my favorite place to read?
4. What are my favorite titles?
5. Who are my favorite authors?
6. What is my dream vacation?
7. What is my favorite color?
8. What is my favorite time of day?
9. What do I do to escape?
10. Where do I go to escape?
11. What is my favorite time of day?
12. What is my favorite time of year/season/month?
13. What do I do to relax?

14. What is my favorite type of music?
15. Who is my favorite musician(s)?
16. What is my favorite dessert?
17. What is my favorite drink?
18. What is my favorite liquor (if I were going to drink)?
19. What is my favorite musical instrument?
20. What are the instruments that I want to learn to play?
21. What makes me cry?
22. What makes me laugh?
23. What do I do for fun?
24. What inspires me?
25. What are 5 things I want to achieve?
26. What is my favorite snack?
27. What is my favorite sport?
28. What is my favorite sport's team?
29. What is my favorite poem?
30. What is my favorite poet?
31. Who do I call when it's going well?
32. Who do I call when it is not going well?
33. Where do I want to travel?
34. What is my favorite flavor of ice cream?
35. What is my favorite brand of ice cream?
36. What do I do for exercise?
37. What is my pet peeve?
38. What is my favorite style of underwear?
39. What is my favorite television show?
40. Why do I like those movies?
41. Why do I like this show?
42. What excites me?
43. What shuts me down?
44. What do I fear?
45. What makes me happy?

46. What makes me smile?
47. Do I prefer sunshine or rain?
48. Where do I seek guidance and information?
49. What do I need?
50. What are my strengths?
51. What are my weaknesses?
52. What is my favorite car?
53. What is my favorite truck/SUV?
54. What is my favorite car color?
55. What is my favorite restaurant?
56. What is my favorite store?
57. What is my favorite pet?
58. What is my ideal profession?
59. What does my mother think I should be?
60. What does it take for my love tank to be full?
61. What do I do when I am sad?
62. What do I do when I am happy?
63. Who would I like to meet and spend time with (public and famous)?
64. How do you know when I am happy?
65. How do I like to be kissed?
66. How do I like to be held?
67. What is my favorite lovemaking position(s)?
68. Why are birthdays so important to me?
69. What do I dream of?
70. What is my definition of success?
71.
72.
73.
74.
75.

The Intensive Retreat for Couples

All About Him

1. What are five of my favorite movies?
2. What is my ideal meal?
3. Where is my favorite place to read?
4. What are my favorite titles?
5. Who are my favorite authors?
6. What is my dream vacation?
7. What is my favorite color?
8. What is my favorite time of day
9. What do I do to escape?
10. Where do I go to escape?
11. What is my favorite time of day?
12. What is my favorite time of year?
13. What do I do to relax?
14. What is my favorite type of music?
15. Who is my favorite musician(s)?
16. What is my favorite dessert?
17. What is my favorite drink?
18. What is my favorite liquor (if I were going to drink)?
19. What is my favorite musical instrument?
20. What are the instruments that I want to learn to play?
21. What makes me cry?
22. What makes me laugh?
23. What do I do for fun?
24. What inspires me?
25. What are 5 things I want to achieve?
26. What is my favorite snack?
27. What is my favorite sport?

28. What is my favorite sport's team?
29. What is my favorite poem?
30. What is my favorite poet?
31. Who do I call when it's going well?
32. Who do I call when it is not going well?
33. Where do I want to travel?
34. What is my favorite flavor of ice cream?
35. What is my favorite brand of ice cream?
36. What do I do for exercise?
37. What is my pet peeve?
38. What is my favorite style of underwear?
39. What is my favorite television show?
40. Why do I like those movies?
41. Why do I like this show?
42. What excites me?
43. What shuts me down?
44. What do I fear?
45. What makes me happy?
46. What makes me smile?
47. Do I prefer sunshine or rain?
48. Where do I seek guidance and information?
49. What do I need?
50. What are my strengths?
51. What are my weaknesses?
52. What is my favorite car?
53. What is my favorite truck/SUV?
54. What is my favorite car color?
55. What is my favorite restaurant?
56. What is my favorite store?
57. What is my favorite pet?
58. What is my ideal profession?
59. What does my mother think I should be?

60. What does it take for my love tank to be full?
61. What do I do when I am sad?
62. What do I do when I am happy?
63. Who would I like to meet and spend time with (public and famous)?
64. How do you know when I am happy?
65. How do I like to be kissed?
66. How do I like to be held?
67. What is my favorite lovemaking position(s)?
68. Why are birthdays so important to me?
69. What do I dream of?
70. What is my definition of success?
71.
72.
73.
74.
75.

Where Are We?

Why Are We Here?

Where are we?

Why are we here?

These questions cause us to evaluate our relationship. The evaluation will reveal that you and your husband are in two different places. No matter how you assess that information, you will discover that you are either a little different or EXTREMELY different. The issue is NOT the difference, rather that you are newly realizing that there are such differences. The second surprise is how major the differences are.

The unspoken, undefined issues can create a physical, spiritual and intimate distance. This distance is the real problem in your marriage.

When you ask and answer 'where are we,' and that answer is immensely different, I am going to help you to reach a place such that you are not so far away. The ability to agree on a location is key to reaching the goal.

Why are we here? At this place in our relationship? Wishing we were elsewhere? Wondering how this happened? To us? What do we do now? How do we return to a great place?

We only need to confess TRUTHFULLY where we are individually to one another so that we can arrive at the goal place.

After we discover our issues, then we will develop a plan for overcoming those obstacles as well as shortening our distance.

Let us start finding out where we are and why we are here.

The Intensive Retreat for Couples

Define marriage. Your personal definition, not the dictionary, nor culture or societal.

_____
_____
_____
_____
_____
_____
_____
_____
_____
_____
_____
_____
_____
_____
_____
_____
_____
_____
_____
_____
_____
_____

Her Workbook

Where are we?

Why are we here?

Share your view of your marriage in its current state.

_____
_____
_____
_____
_____
_____
_____
_____
_____
_____
_____
_____
_____
_____
_____
_____

The Intensive Retreat for Couples

Share your desires for your marriage.

What do you want your marriage to be?

_____
_____
_____
_____
_____
_____
_____
_____
_____
_____
_____
_____
_____
_____
_____
_____
_____

Her Workbook

What is your marriage missing?

What is the most difficult part of your marriage?

_____
_____
_____
_____
_____
_____
_____
_____
_____
_____
_____
_____
_____
_____
_____

The Intensive Retreat for Couples

What is great about your marriage?

_____
_____
_____
_____
_____
_____
_____
_____
_____
_____
_____
_____
_____
_____
_____
_____
_____
_____
_____
_____

Her Workbook

Why did you choose to engage in this intensive study?

How did you come to agree to this study and retreat?

_____
_____
_____
_____
_____
_____
_____
_____
_____
_____
_____
_____
_____
_____
_____

The Intensive Retreat for Couples

What actual event caused you to arrive here? What was the 'last straw'?

_____
_____
_____
_____
_____
_____
_____
_____
_____
_____
_____
_____
_____
_____
_____
_____
_____
_____
_____
_____
_____

Her Workbook

What happened when you mentioned this retreat to your husband?

Were there conditions or bargains made in order to arrive here at this retreat?

The Intensive Retreat for Couples

Grade your relationship.

What is the ideal grade your relationship should have?

What was the highest grade your relationship has ever had?

What does it take to arrive at the ideal place for your marriage?

_____
_____
_____
_____
_____
_____
_____
_____
_____
_____
_____
_____
_____
_____
_____
_____
_____

The Ideal Marriage

God invented marriage for man and woman so that each person would have some help through God's assignments in your life. God created marriage for the fulfillment of the covenant between a man and a woman. This covenant started with God and still includes God. The Ideal Marriage honors God and holds to His commands, keeps His covenant, facilitates His work and shares His love with each and others.

The ideal marriage encourages and forgives. It studies and seeks God for righteousness and direction. It builds and supports. It is a bridge and a covering. Ideal marriages are happy, healthy, and whole. Ideal marriages love, foster healing, and keep no record of wrongs. The ideal marriage is harmonious and is romantic.

The ideal marriage is made up of two ideal people who are imperfect and flawed but has the BEST intentions for the other person.

The way to have an ideal marriage is to be an ideal person.

Everyone who is married has a definition of an ideal marriage. Have you shared your definition with your spouse through your actions, words and deeds? Through your attitude? Your intentions? The key to the ideal marriage: YOU!

The Ideal Marriage is based on who you are individually. Because of that, we need to investigate our unique definitions of an ideal marriage and how we personally contribute to that definition.

Be sure to understand that it is hard to require someone to do something that you are not willing to do personally. Further, you have greater influence when you demonstrate the expected behavior—consistently.

The Intensive Retreat for Couples

How do I define The Ideal Marriage?

How will I communicate my definition of my ideal marriage to my husband?

What does it take to reach that definition in my marriage?

_____
_____
_____
_____
_____
_____
_____
_____
_____
_____
_____
_____
_____
_____
_____
_____
_____
_____
_____

What is my daily schedule?

What time belongs to my husband?

The Intensive Retreat for Couples

What portion of my life does my husband know?

If you died, what would your husband find out about you?

Is there anything that would embarrass your husband?

Are you welcoming with your tone when you speak with your husband?

Are you excited about the communication between you and your husband?

How would you like to achieve the ideal relationship?

What time does that require?

What activities does that entail?

What level of communication is needed for the ideal marriage to be reached?

_____
_____
_____
_____
_____
_____
_____
_____
_____
_____
_____
_____
_____
_____
_____
_____
_____

Her Workbook

What motivates you to be the ideal wife?

What can you do to motivate your husband to be a better husband?

The Intensive Retreat for Couples

What stops your marriage from being ideal?

Communication

Communication is defined as the imparting or interchange of thoughts, opinions, or information by speech, writing, or signs.

By definition, communication requires action.

Communication means that you are engaged with the other person, actively and consistently. Communication is key to relationships. Your husband needs that communication. Further, your husband or yourself may THRIVE on that communication. Communication is an investment. Communication validates the other person's needs. Communication clears up misunderstandings. Communication is the answer to most issues in your relationship.

How will you communicate? What will you communicate? In what tone will you communicate? In what location will you communicate? Who will hear you communicate?

When I said, "Your communication is my air, by which I live and off of which I thrive." He was speechless. While he never really responded, his behavior demonstrated that he had no clue what I meant, what I needed, nor why I said it.

The level of communication you need to be successful is defined by your husband, not by you. The communication he needs is defined by him. You are designed to meet that need.

Successful communication is built on transparency. Transparency builds trust. Trust makes communication easier. When you trust the words, actions and deeds of the other person, love is easier to do and be. It is easier to love someone who does not lie to you and who tells you the whole truth. Those are two different details.

Communication is not blind and is not dumb. Remember that communication is not love, so it keeps score. Communication keeps track and has an outstanding memory of the not so great communication misunderstandings.

The Intensive Retreat for Couples

Great communication is a decision. It is a choice. It is no accident when you elect not to communicate clearly with your husband. It is not an accident when you elect to lie or hide something from your husband, especially when you are asked directly about the matter.

Do you want to be married or do you want to be private?

Her Workbook

Define what you expect of your husband for communication.

What can your husband expect of you?

The Intensive Retreat for Couples

What do you do to communicate with your husband?

What happens when you do not communicate with your husband?

_____
_____
_____
_____
_____
_____
_____
_____
_____
_____
_____
_____
_____
_____
_____
_____
_____
_____
_____
_____

Her Workbook

What happens when your husband does not communicate with you?

What happens when your do not hear from your husband for an extended period of time?

The Intensive Retreat for Couples

What would happen if you discovered that your husband kept as many secrets as you, told as many lies as you, and withheld as much information as you?

How would you feel?

How would you respond?

_____
_____
_____
_____
_____
_____
_____
_____
_____
_____
_____
_____
_____
_____
_____
_____
_____
_____
_____
_____

Her Workbook

What does it take for you to stop the lack of communication?

How could you change in such a manner that your husband would embrace your commitment to communicate?

Has your husband given up on your ability to communicate with him?

_____
_____
_____
_____
_____
_____
_____
_____
_____
_____
_____
_____
_____
_____
_____
_____

The Intensive Retreat for Couples

Can You Hear Me?

Active Listening

Listening and hearing have been proven different. However, we treat them the same. Verizon made the question: "Can you hear me now?" famous a few years ago. It is a source of hurt in most relationships and has been this way for years.

Listening is an active practice designed to hear and understand what your husband has said. Gage defines the difference as listening incites action. Action should result from listening. Hearing is a passive behavior, which does not require anything. Hearing may not even require a conversation.

Listening is a verb, requiring action; expecting results. Active listening involves asking questions and gaining clarity. Active listening warrants follow through and more dialogue.

Listening involves intimacy and attention to detail. Listening and acting on what you are listening to should bring you closer.

Technically, listening and hearing are synonymous. Often used interchangeably as needed, however, in order to close the gap between you and your husband, action is required. If nothing ever happens after a conversation, you are not listening. Note for the speaker: please understand that effective listening requires effective delivery.

This means that you cannot leave ANY conversation saying or believing that 'he knows what I mean' or 'he knows what I meant.' If you did not SAY it out loud, then words were not heard! Your husband cannot take action on something you never said. If you are not willing to share, then you DO NOT want the action you <u>thought</u> about.

Effective conversation, also known as communication, is only achieved when you are able to say what you are feeling or thinking or dreaming of.

It is imperative we do not claim effective communication when we blame him for ineffective listening.

The Intensive Retreat for Couples

The listener should not need an interpreter to know what the speaker means. That can be annoying, particularly when the listener is held accountable for what you meant but never said.

This is critical when you are trying to eliminate the space between the two of you.

Can you hear me now is only a valid question if you are sharing effectively.

Last thing on this serious topic, which is the source of most of your fights: live by the same rules which you expect others to live by. You cannot request transparent, honest communication, active listening, and action-based responses when you lie, share half the story and do nothing about the needs or interests of your husband.

Her Workbook

Do you feel that your husband hears and responds to you as you need?

If not, why not?

If yes, is it consistent?

_____
_____
_____
_____
_____
_____
_____
_____
_____
_____
_____
_____
_____
_____
_____
_____
_____

The Intensive Retreat for Couples

What does it mean to you when your husband hears you?

Her Workbook

What do you want to your husband to do to show you that he heard you?

How do you feel when your husband does not hear or does not take action on what he heard?

_____
_____
_____
_____
_____
_____
_____
_____
_____
_____
_____
_____
_____
_____
_____
_____
_____

The Intensive Retreat for Couples

Do you withhold valuable information which could equip your husband to be better?

If so, why?

___
___
___
___
___
___
___
___
___
___
___
___
___
___
___
___
___
___

Her Workbook

How could you make your husband feel more valuable?

The Intensive Retreat for Couples

What are you thinking about when your husband is talking?

What are you doing when your husband is talking?

Are you hoping he would just shut up?

Are you just waiting on your opportunity to respond without really listening to what your husband actually said?

_____
_____
_____
_____
_____
_____
_____
_____
_____
_____
_____
_____
_____
_____

Her Workbook

The Intensive Retreat for Couples

What would make you engage your husband better?

___

Trust

As we enter into the subject of trust, I am hoping that you decide to do whatever it takes for your husband to trust you.

Trust as a noun is the reliance on the integrity, strength, ability, surety of that person or thing; confidence. Trust is related to security, certainty, belief, assurance, and faith. "Trust implies instructive unquestioning belief in and reliance upon something."

Trust is valuable and is foundational in any relationship. There are elements which build trust and there are other elements which erode that trust. Our job in our relationships is to guard the trust our husband has for us. Likewise, do our best to not erode the trust that you have with your husband.

The trust, once eroded or lost, is hard to regain; not impossible, but really hard.

Trust is maintained similar to way it is earned. Be clear in your communication. Be transparent in your dealings. Be open to your husband when he questions or when he asks you. Tell the truth and this avails you to certain consequences. Make decisions based on how your husband will respond if he knows or will find out.

Your husband's security is based on what you do and do not do. It is your job to offer him the ability to trust you. It is your responsibility to insure that he trusts you. Trust can be achieved after it is lost based on your attitude about the activity which led to the distrust.

You may be thinking how can that be? Well here are some suggestions:

1. Share the passwords to all of your accounts.
2. Delete all contact information of past relationships.
3. Do not open new email addresses at work or otherwise which you do not plan to use to email your husband.
4. Do not open a separate credit cards or bank accounts without the knowledge of your husband.

5. Do not connect socially on social media even if it is for business purposes if you are attracted to the person in any manner.
6. Share times when you are tempted by another man, either visually or mentally, or otherwise.
7. Be honest about your thoughts, needs or desires.
8. Do not become defensive about any questions your husband asks you about your whereabouts, behavior, and activities.
9. Remember that trust is mutual. Protect it with your communication and connections.
10. Ask for forgiveness. Keep asking until you are forgiven. Do not become defensive nor quit while you are waiting to be restored.

Trust should be like the oxygen to a relationship. Without trust, the relationship will have a hard time sustaining.

Trusting.

Trusted.

Trust.

Define trust and your trust philosophy.

How valuable is trust to you between you and your husband?

Does your husband trust you?

Do you trust your husband?

Her Workbook

What do you do to earn the trust of your husband?

The Intensive Retreat for Couples

What do you to maintain the trust of your husband?

_____
_____
_____
_____
_____
_____
_____
_____
_____
_____
_____
_____
_____
_____
_____
_____
_____
_____
_____
_____
_____
_____

Her Workbook

What do you to erode the trust of your husband?

Why do you continue to erode that trust?

The Intensive Retreat for Couples

Is it important for your husband to trust you?

Why or why not?

_____
_____
_____
_____
_____
_____
_____
_____
_____
_____
_____
_____
_____
_____
_____
_____
_____
_____
_____
_____

Her Workbook

If your trust was breached, what does it take to earn it back?

If you were the one who has to be forgiven, what would you do because of what you did?

_____
_____
_____
_____
_____
_____
_____
_____
_____
_____
_____
_____
_____
_____
_____
_____
_____

The Intensive Retreat for Couples

What does trust and communication have in common?

How did you reach that philosophy?

_____
_____
_____
_____
_____
_____
_____
_____
_____
_____
_____
_____
_____
_____
_____
_____
_____
_____

Her Workbook

Does your husband cause you to not trust him?

What happens/happened?

___

The Intensive Retreat for Couples

Can you put your phone facing up and share your lock pattern and voicemail passwords?

Can your husband do it as well?

Can you share all of your social media user names and passwords with your husband?

Can your husband share them with you?

The Intensive Retreat for Couples

What would happen if you picked up the wrong phone when you left for work?

Will you still be married when you get home?

Her Workbook

Are you worthy of your husband's trust?

Would you trust you?

The Intensive Retreat for Couples

When you are concerned about your husband's behavior and activities, what do you do?

_____
_____
_____
_____
_____
_____
_____
_____
_____
_____
_____
_____
_____
_____
_____
_____
_____
_____
_____
_____

Her Workbook

Are you transparent with your husband?

Do you make your husband beg and probe for information?

_____
_____
_____
_____
_____
_____
_____
_____
_____
_____
_____
_____
_____
_____
_____
_____

The Intensive Retreat for Couples

Are you completely honest with your husband?

Why not?

What does it take to be honest with your husband?

_____
_____
_____
_____
_____
_____
_____
_____
_____
_____
_____
_____
_____
_____
_____
_____
_____
_____
_____
_____

Her Workbook

Are you causing your husband to question or second guess your honesty?

Why?

What can you do to stop his fears?

_____
_____
_____
_____
_____
_____
_____
_____
_____
_____
_____
_____
_____
_____
_____

The Intensive Retreat for Couples

Are you able to do everything on the suggestion list about regaining or/and maintaining your husband's trust?

___

Her Workbook

If your trust is eroded, how long can your relationship continue to exist?

The Intensive Retreat for Couples

Write a letter to your husband. Either thank him or apologize for the level of the trust in your relationship.

Love

You love him with all of your heart and you want him to love you back with that same amount of zeal. I know because it is hard to understand what they do not understand about love. As a woman, you understand love and we do not run out of it. God is the replenisher of that love and we know that so we are deliberately elaborate in that love, but somehow we cannot expect the same.

Our husband seems to intentionally withhold from us the love we desire and deserve. This is far from acceptable, however there is hope. Consider your husband. Keep in mind that men are different and it seems like an excuse and we are tired of hearing it but the good news is that we know that he is different from us as women and that is actually a good thing.

Keep focused on God. Remember that God sent you to this man. For that reason, you are to keep God's commands to love one another. There is a way to get the love you want from him but it is outlandishly different from how your imagined. Do not lose heart. Love is not impossible, however the work is different for him.

Define love for him from your perspective. When you say to him, "Why don't you love you?" what does that mean? How do you want him to respond? How do you intend to help him learn to love you?

Defend your need for love but this not a combat zone. Show him how to love through demonstration rather than lecture and instruction. Easier said than done in your mind because your rationale is that this man leads dozens of people or manages millions of dollars in revenue or travels the globe to provide for us. So you think that he is smart enough to love you? He is smart enough to love you but the same with all of his other credentials, he was taught and trained. Demonstrate your love through loving him. He defines love differently than you. But you already know that.

Share your heart with him. Keep the love tank full (Chapman). Continue to pray for him and all that he does. Remind him that you want him and need his love. Remind him with roles and deeds that you are there for forever—nothing short thereof.

The Intensive Retreat for Couples

He loves you. He is challenged in showing you consistently by your definition. We will work to find a means for understanding.

Her Workbook

Define love.

Do you and your husband agree on the definition?

_____
_____
_____
_____
_____
_____
_____
_____
_____
_____
_____
_____
_____
_____
_____
_____
_____

The Intensive Retreat for Couples

Do you love your husband?

Why?

_____
_____
_____
_____
_____
_____
_____
_____
_____
_____
_____
_____
_____
_____
_____
_____
_____
_____

Her Workbook

Does your husband love you?

How do you know?

_____
_____
_____
_____
_____
_____
_____
_____
_____
_____
_____
_____
_____
_____
_____
_____

The Intensive Retreat for Couples

What is your love language? (www.**5lovelanguages**.com/profile)

Were you surprised about this love language?

Are you hard to love?

Why or why not?

The Intensive Retreat for Couples

Is your husband hard to love?

Why or why not?

Is it easy for you to love your husband?

_____
_____
_____
_____
_____
_____
_____
_____
_____
_____
_____
_____
_____
_____
_____
_____
_____
_____

Her Workbook

Are you in love with your husband?

Is your husband in love with you?

How do you know?

The Intensive Retreat for Couples

How does authentic love affect your relationship?

How does it help with responses and behavior?

_____
_____
_____
_____
_____
_____
_____
_____
_____
_____
_____
_____
_____
_____
_____
_____
_____
_____

Do others see the love you share with your husband?

The Intensive Retreat for Couples

What makes the love between you and your husband special?

What is significant about your love?

The Intensive Retreat for Couples

How do you explain and describe the love you have for your husband?

_____
_____
_____
_____
_____
_____
_____
_____
_____
_____
_____
_____
_____
_____
_____
_____
_____
_____
_____
_____

How would you explain the following verse: "Love covers a multitude of sins?"

The Intensive Retreat for Couples

How do you keep the love alive and fresh in your relationship?

What do you do when the love seems weak or faint?

The Intensive Retreat for Couples

Describe some 'just because' love moments or behaviors.

Her Workbook

Describe how you demonstrate love for your husband.

The Intensive Retreat for Couples

What can you do to show your husband more love?

_____
_____
_____
_____
_____
_____
_____
_____
_____
_____
_____
_____
_____
_____
_____
_____
_____
_____
_____
_____

Her Workbook

What can your husband do to show you more love?

The Intensive Retreat for Couples

Does your husband tell you that he loves you enough?

Do you share your loving feelings with your husband enough for him?

The Intensive Retreat for Couples

How do your childhood relationship experiences with your parents affect your relationship?

_____
_____
_____
_____
_____
_____
_____
_____
_____
_____
_____
_____
_____
_____
_____
_____
_____
_____

What does love make you do differently?

The Intensive Retreat for Couples

Write your husband a love letter.

_____
_____
_____
_____
_____
_____
_____
_____
_____
_____
_____
_____
_____
_____
_____
_____
_____
_____
_____
_____

Respect

Respect is how he spells love. This has been a mystery since the creation of man because we have overlooked it for that same span of time. Ephesians 5:33 reads, "However each one of you also must love his wife as he loves himself, and the wife must respect her husband."

While there are not explicit instructions on how a wife is to respect a husband, we can arrive there by several mechanisms. Respect is at the foundation a part of honor, adoration, understanding and trust. For us, respect is as vague as love is for him.

God wants us to work at revealing this otherwise mystery to each other. Respect is required by God to your husband. It is one of the vaguest terms ever constructed. Respect is hard to understand and harder to execute. Respect is different for each man as well, so what works for your neighbor's husband does not work at your house.

The most interesting thing about respect is that your husband cannot be depended upon to share with you what his definition of respect is or how to achieve it. It may seem like you are always finding out what is disrespectful to him, but in a reactive manner, rather than a proactive, safe environment, where good respect can be practiced.

Respect lifts his head and creates a powerful disposition in that he is able to function with the respect he desires. Respect seems like your approval. When we respect him, it translates into 'I believe in you, husband.' Respect implies that you regard him highly. This feeling for him is parallel to our need for love.

The respect he needs is like the love we need. Essential. Necessary. Required. Demanded. Critical. Proactive.

How do I learn to respect him if he does not help me to know how to respect him? I understand your feelings and this could lead to disrespect and confusion. I have a suggestion: The Golden Rule: do unto him what you have him do unto you.

1. Come home at a respectable time. In most cities, malls, restaurants, and other venues are closing at 9 pm. Go home.
2. Do not come into the house talking on the telephone.
3. Give/offer him your undivided attention.
4. Let him finish his sentences and thoughts.
5. Listen to understand rather than finding fault. Present a solution to what you consider an as issue.
6. Figure out what is important to him. Ask enough questions to understand what makes him tick. Interesting facts. What does he share with his friends? What keeps him awake while you are sleeping?
7. Understand his interests. Hobbies. His work. His addictions. His fears. His favorites. Use this information to relate to him.
8. Take inventory of his family life; his background is essential to understanding his definition of respect.
9. Find out who he respects and why he respects him or her so that you can how he measures that respect.
10. Keep him first right after God. Remind him that no matter what you have or achieve or know, he is still most important.
11. Remind yourself why you fell in love and why you are in each other's lives in the first place.

Respect is an ongoing challenge. Because you have a mind, a heart, and a personality, this world can encourage you to disrespect your husband because of what you know and what you have and what you can be without him. The world encourages our independence which could easily lead to disrespect of your husband.

Respecting your husband does not mean that you are less than who God created you to be. Your ability to respect him speaks volumes about the woman you really are.

You respect God so you are obedient and because you are obedient, you respect your husband.

Her Workbook

How will your respect your husband?

The Intensive Retreat for Couples

How have you disrespected him in the past?

What did you do to correct that disrespect?

Why has it been hard to respect your husband?

Did you share your feelings with him?

What was his response?

_____
_____
_____
_____
_____
_____
_____
_____
_____
_____
_____
_____
_____
_____
_____
_____
_____

The Intensive Retreat for Couples

Have you asked God for forgiveness?

Have you asked for your husband's forgiveness?

Has your husband forgiven you for your disrespect of him?

Have you forgiven yourself?

Who do you know who consistently respects her husband enough to use her as a mentor and sounding board?

_____
_____
_____
_____
_____
_____
_____
_____
_____
_____
_____
_____
_____
_____
_____
_____
_____

The Intensive Retreat for Couples

Are there classes or workshops that you can attend which help facilitate the process of respect?

_____
_____
_____
_____
_____
_____
_____
_____
_____
_____
_____
_____
_____
_____
_____
_____
_____
_____
_____
_____

Her Workbook

Did you ever respect him?

What changed?

The Intensive Retreat for Couples

What do you think he could do to regain your respect?

Should respect be earned or given? Explain why?

Her Workbook

Does he deserve your respect?

Why or why not?

_____
_____
_____
_____
_____
_____
_____
_____
_____
_____
_____
_____
_____
_____
_____
_____
_____

The Intensive Retreat for Couples

What has been the consequence of your disrespect?

How have you handled that?

_____
_____
_____
_____
_____
_____
_____
_____
_____
_____
_____
_____
_____
_____
_____
_____
_____

Respond to the following statement: "Her respect is my oxygen."

How can you make this work in your marriage?

The Intensive Retreat for Couples

Does your pride prevent you from being respectful to your husband?

How can you rectify that pride?

_____
_____
_____
_____
_____
_____
_____
_____
_____
_____
_____
_____
_____
_____
_____
_____
_____
_____

What do you see as your reward for being respectful of your husband?

The Intensive Retreat for Couples

Write a letter of apology for any time(s) when you have been disrespectful.

Divorce Explored

Divorce should not be an option. It is beyond the last resort! Divorce is permanent solution to often temporary situations. Divorce leaves scars. Divorce should be viewed as a non-option!

The ripple effect of divorce is huge—bigger than you may ever realize. Divorces are becoming more frequent—almost popular. The problem is divorce does not end your relationship. Remember if you have children, you will need to communicate with that spouse because of the children.

Before you reach for divorce as a solution, interview some people who are divorced, and at least one man. Keep in mind that divorce is not the only solution; often it is not the best solution.

Divorces happen because pride is overwhelming. Someone needs to say 'I do not want this to end' and 'what does it take to make this work?' Someone needs to listen to her heart and someone needs to realize that this may be solvable if and only if you are willing to do some work—some major, some minor.

Visit the family who has endured divorce and ask yourself which life you would prefer. Can your situation be overcome? Can your situation be solved with some different activities?

Is your situation bad enough to end this and possibly start over with someone else? Consider carefully the use of that option. The feelings which are hurt are going to be your children.

Can this be fixed? If no, then divorce. Be ready for the ugly. If yes, then put all else aside and authentically and genuinely work on your relationship and improve the health of your marriage.

Lastly, stop using divorce as a threat to influence change in your marriage.

The Intensive Retreat for Couples

Can you live without your husband?

Are you going to regret the decision of divorce?

_____
_____
_____
_____
_____
_____
_____
_____
_____
_____
_____
_____
_____
_____
_____
_____
_____
_____
_____
_____

Her Workbook

Can your issues be solved?

How are you making that determination?

What 'extra' does it take to solve them?

_____
_____
_____
_____
_____
_____
_____
_____
_____
_____
_____
_____
_____
_____
_____
_____
_____

The Intensive Retreat for Couples

Will you be able to parent amicably?

How are you going to feel/react about someone having influence in raising your children, especially when it challenges the agreement you and your husband made previously?

___
___
___
___
___
___
___
___
___
___
___
___
___
___
___
___
___
___

Her Workbook

Can you see your husband with someone else without wanting your husband or becoming sick about your situation?

___

The Intensive Retreat for Couples

Will you use the court system to make your husband 'pay' for what he has done or not done in your marriage?

_____
_____
_____
_____
_____
_____
_____
_____
_____
_____
_____
_____
_____
_____
_____
_____
_____
_____
_____

Can you walk away with no regrets or without questions?

The Intensive Retreat for Couples

Document your family history: previous divorces, never marrieds and the length of existing marriages, along with a health grade of each marriage.

Will your divorce challenge your families?

___

Her Workbook

How are your children going to feel?

How will this impact your friends? Church friends? Social circles?

_____
_____
_____
_____
_____
_____
_____
_____
_____
_____
_____
_____
_____
_____
_____
_____

The Intensive Retreat for Couples

Is your situation life threatening?

Are your circumstances as bad as they can get?

_____
_____
_____
_____
_____
_____
_____
_____
_____
_____
_____
_____
_____
_____
_____
_____
_____
_____
_____
_____

Fighting Fair

Conflict is defined as a fight, battle, or struggle, especially a prolonged struggle; strife, as a noun. Conflict is going to happen; you will not agree on all things at all times. However, the use of conflict as a noun rather than a verb is the start of some relational success.

Do not purpose to FIGHT. There will be disagreements but resolve can be present as well.

All fights should be FAIR. If there has to be a fight, then decide. DECIDE to fight fairly. Often I find that when we are hurt, hurting, and maybe even angry, we fight like we do not love and much less like our husband that we are fighting.

Rules of Fighting Fair:

1. Decide that there is a resolve that can be reached.
2. Decide to reach a resolve with a win-win attitude.
3. Do not design a solution where your husband loses.
4. Stick to the matter at hand. Do not add to the issue and do not bring up unrelated, old issues.
5. Control your attitude. Remain calm while speaking and listening.
6. Pray before, during and after your discussion.
7. Be honest with your facts, feelings, and opinions about the matter.
8. Listen to your husband!
9. Remember you love this man. Your husband loves you and you love him. Treat your husband like you love him.
10. Focus on what God would want you to do.
11. How can we reach a resolve and each party can feel edified?
12. As you work on the solution, remember this relationship is for a lifetime; this situation is temporary.
13. Research the best solution.
14. Uncover how this developed initially, so that we can prevent this from happening again.

15. Write down your resolution so that you can keep your word.

When you solve conflict responsibly, you will feel better. You will be more comfortable in your relationship when neither party has lost or leaves the conflict hurting or broken. Great conflict resolution leads to great communication and a greater relationship.

Her Workbook

Do you pick fights?

Do you start most of the fights?

The Intensive Retreat for Couples

Do you try to avoid fights?

How do you try to avoid fighting?

Her Workbook

What are most of your fights about?

The Intensive Retreat for Couples

How long do your fights last?

How have your fights ended?

Do you feel differently about your husband after a fight?

Does that feeling depend on the outcome of the fight?

The Intensive Retreat for Couples

Who is the reconciler in the relationship?

Are you a peacemaker?

Do you have the ability to be a peacemaker?

What does it take to be a peacemaker?

___
___
___
___
___
___
___
___
___
___
___
___
___
___
___
___
___
___
___

Her Workbook

Have you ever studied conflict resolution?

Are you using any of the principles you learned in the class?

The Intensive Retreat for Couples

How do you seek to understand your husband?

How do you seek to be understood?

How would you like to be understood?

___

Her Workbook

Can you fight and still love your husband?

The Intensive Retreat for Couples

Is it a challenge to respect your husband after a fight?

Her Workbook

Do you apologize when you are wrong or at fault?

Is it easy?

Why or why not?

_____
_____
_____
_____
_____
_____
_____
_____
_____
_____
_____
_____
_____
_____
_____
_____
_____

The Intensive Retreat for Couples

Do you consider yourself easy to get along with?

Why or why not?

_____
_____
_____
_____
_____
_____
_____
_____
_____
_____
_____
_____
_____
_____
_____
_____
_____
_____

Her Workbook

Can you forget about the fight once it is resolved?

Why or why not?

The Intensive Retreat for Couples

How long does it take you to forgive your husband when you have been hurt?

Does your husband have to beg for your forgiveness?

Does your husband have to bargain for your forgiveness?

_____
_____
_____
_____
_____
_____
_____
_____
_____
_____
_____
_____
_____
_____
_____
_____
_____
_____
_____
_____

Intimacy

Intimacy as a woman does not always mean sex. Intimacy is expressed and felt through many mediums: conversation, holding hands, sitting next to your husband, or a candlelight dinner. Intimacy can be communicated in a glance, a touch, a hug, and a dance.

Intimacy is required for the health of your wellness and the measure of the health of your relationship. As women, we consider intimacy a grade of love from your husband.

Intimacy is defined differently for each person. If sex is his definition, then you need to come to an agreement about what that means.

Intimacy is necessary and essential for a healthy relationship even if you do not completely agree on the definition. You need to remember that both of you needs the other person. This is critical to the health and wellness of your relationship.

Intimacy needs to be treated carefully. This is not a place to pick a fight on purpose. I am always concerned about us as women using intimacy, particularly sex, to make our voice heard.

One married woman told me that she had exercised her right to serve her husband with economic sanctions. Initially, I did not understand. What I then understood that she was withholding sex as a punishment. Later, I learned that he was unfaithful and then they divorced. The intimacy between a couple is sensitive and does not deserve tampering or mishandling.

1 Corinthians 7:2-6 The Message (MSG)
2-6 Certainly—but only within a certain context. It's good for a man to have a wife, and for a woman to have a husband. Sexual drives are strong, but marriage is strong enough to contain them and provide for a balanced and fulfilling sexual life in a world of sexual disorder. The marriage bed must be a place of mutuality—the husband seeking to satisfy his wife, the wife seeking to satisfy her husband. Marriage is not a place to "stand up for your rights." Marriage is a decision to serve the other, whether in bed or out. Abstaining from sex is permissible for a period of time if you both agree to it, and if it's for the purposes

of prayer and fasting—but only for such times. Then come back together again. Satan has an ingenious way of tempting us when we least expect it. I'm not, understand, commanding these periods of abstinence—only providing my best counsel if you should choose them.

Intimacy needs to be managed carefully, given its required undivided attention, and never neglected. Intimacy should be a comforting place and an exciting place of retreat. Intimacy is a place that we should anticipate enjoying with the person who we love. Likewise, intimacy is not for negotiation. Intimacy is not about making deals and bargaining and bartering. Intimacy involves giving the other person the most vulnerable parts of ourselves. Complete intimacy includes receiving the other person openly, willingly and without prejudice.

Intimacy is a closeness that should not be sacrificed under any conditions. We should protect the intimacy of our relationship. We should value it and remember why we like the intimacy we share.

We need to learn how to convey our need for intimacy with our husbands. Likewise, we need to understand how to mitigate the damage the lack of intimacy may cause.

Her Workbook

Are you having enough sex?

Are you having sex often enough?

The Intensive Retreat for Couples

What is missing from your intimacy?

What needs to improve to satisfy your intimacy needs?

What works for you now?

What do you want more of?

How do you share what you need more of with your husband?

___
___
___
___
___
___
___
___
___
___
___
___
___
___
___
___
___

How does your husband define intimacy?

How are your definitions different?

How do you manage those differences?

The Intensive Retreat for Couples

What are the areas of your relationship which influence your intimacy levels?

Are these areas which you contribute to the strain on your intimacy (i.e. behavior, attitude, etc.)?

_____
_____
_____
_____
_____
_____
_____
_____
_____
_____
_____
_____
_____
_____
_____
_____
_____
_____
_____

Her Workbook

What area(s) of your relationship does your husband contribute to the decrease and absence of intimacy?

Have you made him aware of those areas?

Do you have a plan/suggestion for how to overcome these areas or solve this issue?

_____
_____
_____
_____
_____
_____
_____
_____
_____
_____
_____
_____
_____
_____
_____
_____
_____

The Intensive Retreat for Couples

Have you been completely honest about your intimate needs?

Why not?

When do you plan on being completely honest?

_____
_____
_____
_____
_____
_____
_____
_____
_____
_____
_____
_____
_____
_____
_____
_____
_____
_____
_____
_____

Her Workbook

Do you use excuses to avoid sex with your husband (i.e. headache, exhaustion, work, children, etc)?

What does it take to abandon these excuses?

The Intensive Retreat for Couples

Do you like your husband?

If not, why not?

_____
_____
_____
_____
_____
_____
_____
_____
_____
_____
_____
_____
_____
_____
_____
_____
_____
_____
_____

Her Workbook

Is intimacy easy?

If not, why not? If so, why?

The Intensive Retreat for Couples

What is the best part of your intimacy?

What is the worst part of your intimacy?

Is there one thing that could revive your intimacy?

_____
_____
_____
_____
_____
_____
_____
_____
_____
_____
_____
_____
_____
_____
_____
_____
_____
_____
_____

Her Workbook

Has either of you been unfaithful?

The Intensive Retreat for Couples

Has the trust been otherwise eroded between the two of you?

If so, what happened?

Can it be resolved?

What does it take to regain each other's trust?

_____
_____
_____
_____
_____
_____
_____
_____
_____
_____
_____
_____
_____
_____
_____
_____
_____

Her Workbook

Describe your best intimate moment(s).

Real or dreamed.

_____
_____
_____
_____
_____
_____
_____
_____
_____
_____
_____
_____
_____
_____
_____
_____

The Intensive Retreat for Couples

What can you do to create an environment where intimacy is easier for both you and your husband?

_____
_____
_____
_____
_____
_____
_____
_____
_____
_____
_____
_____
_____
_____
_____
_____
_____
_____
_____
_____
_____

A Better Marriage

You Can Do This

You are here because you want a better marriage. You are here because you want to fix your marriage. You want to be a better wife. You want to have a better husband. You want to have a better home life. You want to like coming home. You want to like coming home to the husband you chose. You want your husband to want to come home to you. You want to a have an affair proof marriage. While that seems impossible, there are things you can do which make it harder for that to happen.

You want a successful relationship and you miss the initial stages of your relationship. You may have even considered divorce, but you really want your marriage because you really love and like your husband. You are still in love with your husband. There are just some relational issues which require your attention.

One of you works longer hours. One of you is too busy to schedule date night. The children take up more time than you imagined. Something is more important than each of you.

What does it take to have a better marriage? What do YOU have to do to have a better marriage? What is your husband complaining about? Have you considered what your husband needs and wants so that you can improve your marriage?

If you do your part totally and completely, then your husband should be influenced to do his part. The law of physics which states for every action, there is an equal and opposite reaction. This same activity exists within relationships. Please respond in love rather than the 'tit for tat' that you are currently using to respond. Most relationships suffer from 'you get me, I get you back.' Please put that down. This is detrimental to the relationship.

Decide to be proactive! What are you going to do to help your relationship? Not what are you going to do if he does something. What are you going to do if he does NOTHING? What are you going to do with

The Intensive Retreat for Couples

YOUR marriage? A Better Marriage comes from within you. You have the availability to change the culture of your relationship.

Remember, for a long time your marriage worked, then something happened and you quit. Maybe it was because he quit or he stopped paying attention to you or you had to compete for his time with the television. Then you stopped cooking or keeping his plate until he got home or you stopped being excited when he called. You waited on him to notice. He never noticed. Then you got mad. Now you are here.

Do you wish that you handled anything differently? If you could change anything, either action or lack thereof, what would you change? How can you be a better wife? Use the time we have to share how you can be a better wife, what would you plan differently for your marriage, and for yourself.

How important is your marriage to you? Based on that level should give you the desire and motivation to improve your relationship.

Choose a better marriage! Choose a better self! Make a decision to be a game changer in your relationship. Be revolutionary! Take your relationship back!

Love more extravagantly than ever.

Choose forgiveness rather than bitterness and unforgiveness.

Share your heart again.

Use 'tit for tat' in the best possible option. When something great happens, do something greater in response.

Be transparent again—more so than ever.

Remember when you were excited when he called.

Resume that excitement and that excited voice—use it again! And again!

Keep equipping him to successfully love you!

Affirm his ability to be your husband.

Use your respect for him to influence him and his heart back to your marriage!

Stop saying things that you will regret!

Stop saying things that you do not mean!

Stop doing things that you will need forgiveness for!

Keep focused on what matters!

Stop keeping quiet when you should be talking!

Remember to start with your best and continue to share your best with your husband!

The Intensive Retreat for Couples

On a scale of 1 to 10, how would you rate your marriage?

How did you arrive at that number?

Where should your marriage be?

Why do you feel that way?

What are you using to judge that number?

_____
_____
_____
_____
_____
_____
_____
_____
_____
_____
_____
_____
_____
_____
_____

Her Workbook

What does it take to get to that ideal number?

Do you need help to get there?

Define help.

_____
_____
_____
_____
_____
_____
_____
_____
_____
_____
_____
_____
_____
_____
_____
_____
_____

The Intensive Retreat for Couples

Are you willing to work for that place?

What will you have to do to make your marriage better?

What are YOU willing to do to make your marriage whole again?

_____
_____
_____
_____
_____
_____
_____
_____
_____
_____
_____
_____
_____
_____
_____
_____
_____
_____
_____

Her Workbook

If God were holding only YOU accountable for this marriage's success, what would He expect YOU to do and to change?

___
___
___
___
___
___
___
___
___
___
___
___
___
___
___
___
___
___

The Intensive Retreat for Couples

Who are you in this marriage?

Are you your best you?

If not, why not?

When are you going to get to the best you?

Is your lack of you causing your marriage to suffer?

_____
_____
_____
_____
_____
_____
_____
_____
_____
_____
_____
_____
_____
_____
_____

Her Workbook

Do you give your best to your husband?

Why not?

What does it take to give your best self to your husband?

Why have you been withholding yourself from your husband?

_____
_____
_____
_____
_____
_____
_____
_____
_____
_____
_____
_____
_____
_____
_____
_____

The Intensive Retreat for Couples

When did you stop investing in your relationship?

Why did you stop investing in your relationship?

When will you resume investing in your relationship?

_____
_____
_____
_____
_____
_____
_____
_____
_____
_____
_____
_____
_____
_____
_____
_____
_____

Her Workbook

What part of your relationship do you miss?

How can you can revive or reintroduce that element back into your relationship?

How did that part of your marriage disappear?

_____
_____
_____
_____
_____
_____
_____
_____
_____
_____
_____
_____
_____
_____
_____
_____

The Intensive Retreat for Couples

Does your husband think that your marriage needs support?

Why does your husband feel that way?

What does your husband think your relationship needs?

How can that need be achieved?

_____
_____
_____
_____
_____
_____
_____
_____
_____
_____
_____
_____
_____
_____
_____
_____
_____
_____

Her Workbook

How can your marriage survive this transition into a great marriage?

_____
_____
_____
_____
_____
_____
_____
_____
_____
_____
_____
_____
_____
_____
_____
_____
_____
_____
_____

The Intensive Retreat for Couples

Does the rest of the world, including your children, get the best of you, which means you do not have any energy for your husband, which would include patience and time?

How can you change that circumstance so that you can give your best to your husband?

_____
_____
_____
_____
_____
_____
_____
_____
_____
_____
_____
_____
_____
_____
_____
_____
_____
_____
_____
_____
_____

Tit for Tat

And other relationship solutions

The Final Charge

Was your marriage ever whole by the definition you are now using? Your marriage is still viable. Your marriage can last forever. Are you willing to do the work that it requires?

It does NOT matter who is to blame or why you have arrived here. You are now focused on your marriage.

Healing is needed at this time. Forgiveness is necessary at this time. Focus is important. Along with all of the elements mentioned in this book, hope and belief is required now. This is an important element as well. Overnight is not an option.

Wisdom is also an outcome in this situation. Your previous absolutes are not viable or reasonable in this situation.

This is NOT the time to employ FORT KNOX. Put down the security measures around your heart and the defensive mechanisms which are natural. In order to reach the place you desire, you cannot afford for your heart to be unpenetrable. At some point, you have to afford him the opportunity to regain the lost trust, the broken covenant, the open neglect, the missing love, or whatever brings you to this place.

You are the woman! Be the woman! The woman with power and profound female proclivity. You are a woman which once held his heart, his mind, and his attention. You can regain that place. Mostly you lost that place in your mind; you are still that woman to him. Be ready to stand for ready relationship. Be clear on what you want. Do not switch or change your mind. Keep your focus.

Once you decide to be married, then remain focused.

The Intensive Retreat for Couples

You are the wife. You hold more power than you realize. Regain that position you once held, that means regain the attractiveness, you always possessed. Physical attractiveness permeates from inside. You have to feel attractive to be attractive. You need to be attractive to believe and fight for your husband. Self-confidence is sexy to him. This is necessary to remain focused in this recovery period.

Consider what you talk about when you have conversations. Is it the household activities or is it your smarts expressed through worldly knowledge that excites him? Remember you are smart. Remind him as well.

Decide that you are going to be your absolute best!

Appendix

Calendar for date nights and special occasions

Marriage Vows

Marriage Goals

Mission, Vision, and Value Statements

Expectations and Heart Rules

Resources

The Intensive Retreat for Couples

Calendar for Date Nights

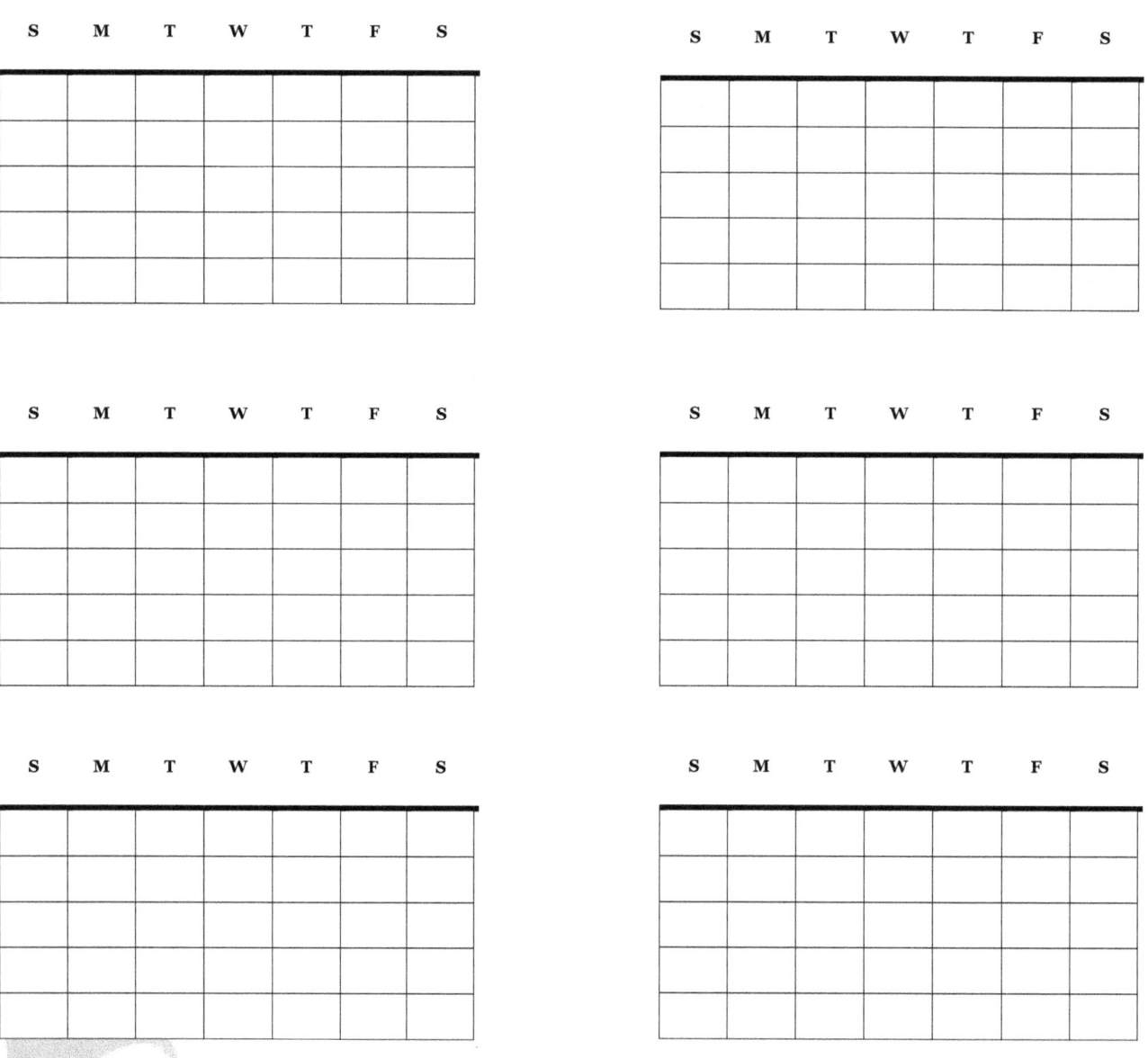

Her Workbook

S	M	T	W	T	F	S

S	M	T	W	T	F	S

S	M	T	W	T	F	S

S	M	T	W	T	F	S

S	M	T	W	T	F	S

S	M	T	W	T	F	S

The Intensive Retreat for Couples

Marriage Vows

I _____ in faith, honesty and love take you ____ as my wedded husband. To share with you in God's plan for our lives together united in Christ. To be a loving helpmate to you with God's help and strength seeking Him always no matter the trial; whether sickness, health; joys or sorrows, till death do us part. I commit to you this day all that I am and all my love; I pledge to you, in the name of our Lord and Savior Jesus Christ. Before Him I offer this ring as a symbol and seal of my love for you and a symbol of unity. I pray to faithfully fulfill my place as your helpmate; to be obedient to God's purpose for me in your life and our lives together. To uphold you in prayer and submit my heart to you; to always be by and on your side, that the presence of the Lord reside in our home, In Jesus Name.

Her Workbook

Marriage Goals

Please establish some goals for your marriage. This is a healthy way to reach a resolve in your marriage. When your needs are met then each spouse feels valued and the marriage will be healthier.

How many date nights each month		
Meals together		
Healthy conversations		
Love		
Respect		
Intimacy and Sex (Frequency, etc)		

The Intensive Retreat for Couples

Mission, Vision, and Value Statements

Your Mission Statement for your marriage.

_____
_____
_____
_____
_____
_____
_____
_____
_____
_____
_____
_____
_____
_____
_____
_____
_____

Your Vision Statement for your marriage.

_____
_____
_____
_____
_____
_____
_____
_____
_____

Your Values for your marriage.

_____
_____
_____
_____
_____
_____
_____
_____
_____
_____

The Intensive Retreat for Couples

Expectations and Heart Rules

What are your marital expectations? What did you expect from your marriage? Are those expectations being met? If not, have you shared this with your husband?

_____
_____
_____
_____
_____
_____
_____
_____
_____
_____
_____
_____
_____
_____
_____
_____
_____
_____
_____
_____

What are your heart rules? (Rules that you live by and what makes your heart happy.)

Resources

From Two to One: The Notebook for the Christian Couple by Minister Onedia N. Gage

Getting Away to Get It Together by Bill and Carolyn Wellons

The Love Dare by Alex and Stephen Kendrick

Saving Your Marriage Before It Starts by Drs. Les and Leslie Parrott

Questions Couples Ask by Drs. Les and Leslie Parrott

Powerful Promises for Every Couple by Jim and Elizabeth George

The Christian Husband by Bob Lepine

The Five Love Languages by Gary Chapman

Kingdom Man by Tony Evans

Kingdom Woman by Tony Evans

The Power of a Praying Wife by Stormie Omartian

The Power of a Praying Husband by Stormie Omartian

The Power of Prayer to Change Your Marriage by Stormie Omartian

The Excellent Wife by Martha Peace

The Excellent Husband by Martha Peace

40 Unforgettable Dates with Your Mate by Dr. Gary and Barbara Rosberg

When God Writes Your Love Story by Eric and Leslie Ludy

Love and Respect by Emerson Eggerichs

Acknowledgments

God, thank You for Your plans for me. Thank You for **The Intensive Retreat for Couples Her Workbook** and choosing me to complete Your project. I just want to please You. Thank You for continuing to anoint me and to invest in me and my gifts, which keep surprising me. Thank You for loving and forgiving me.

Hillary and Nehemiah, thank you for supporting me and my endeavors. Thank you for loving me, especially when I do nothing without a pen and a clipboard, thank you for enduring my late nights, your ideas, the sounding board, the love and the support. Thank you for celebrating our legacy.

To my prayer partners and to my accountability partners, thank you for the long talks and the powerful prayers and the encouragement.

To the women who this will reach and empower and touch and affect, may these words empower you and help you fervently seek God and reach some resolve. May you be inspired to achieve your goals and dreams. May you enhance your relationship with God so that your other relationships will also improve. May you enhance your self-esteem through prayer and studying. May you have courage and peace. Share love the best you can until you can share love without reservation.

The Intensive Retreat for Couples

Her Workbook

ABOUT THE HELPER

Minister Onedia N. Gage believes in the study of God's word. She wants women to have the help she wanted and needed as a former wife so that you can grow with your mate. She hopes that you will seek God for a closer relationship so that you can have a closer relationship with your mate.

Take her advice and testimony seriously. Her experience is invaluable. Please use this to reach God. This relationship is ordained by God. Protect it as such.

Minister Onedia invites you to share her study at her retreats for couples. Minister Onedia would like to pray for and with you. Please contact her via email onediagage@onediagage.com

Via twitter @onediangage, on facebook.com/onedia-gage-ministries and phone 512-715-GAGE (4243).

www.youtube.com/onediagage

www.blogtalkradio.com/onediagage

The Intensive Retreat for Couples

Her Workbook

Preacher ♦ Prayer Warrior ♦ Coach

To invite Rev. Gage to preach, coach, teach, and pray, Please contact us at

@onediangage (twitter) ♦ onediagage@onediagage.com ♦ facebook.com/onediagage

youtube.com/onediagage ♦ blogtalkradio.com/onediagage ♦ www.onediagage.com

The Intensive Retreat for Couples

Publishing

Do you have a book you want to write, but do not know what to do?

Do you have a book you need to publish but do not know how to start?

Would publishing move your career forward?

Let us help

onediagage@purpleink.net ♦ www.purpleink.net

713.705.5530

512.715.4243

www.ingramcontent.com/pod-product-compliance
Lightning Source LLC
Chambersburg PA
CBHW080542170426
43195CB00016B/2651